To Wiktoria, Anna & Amelia,

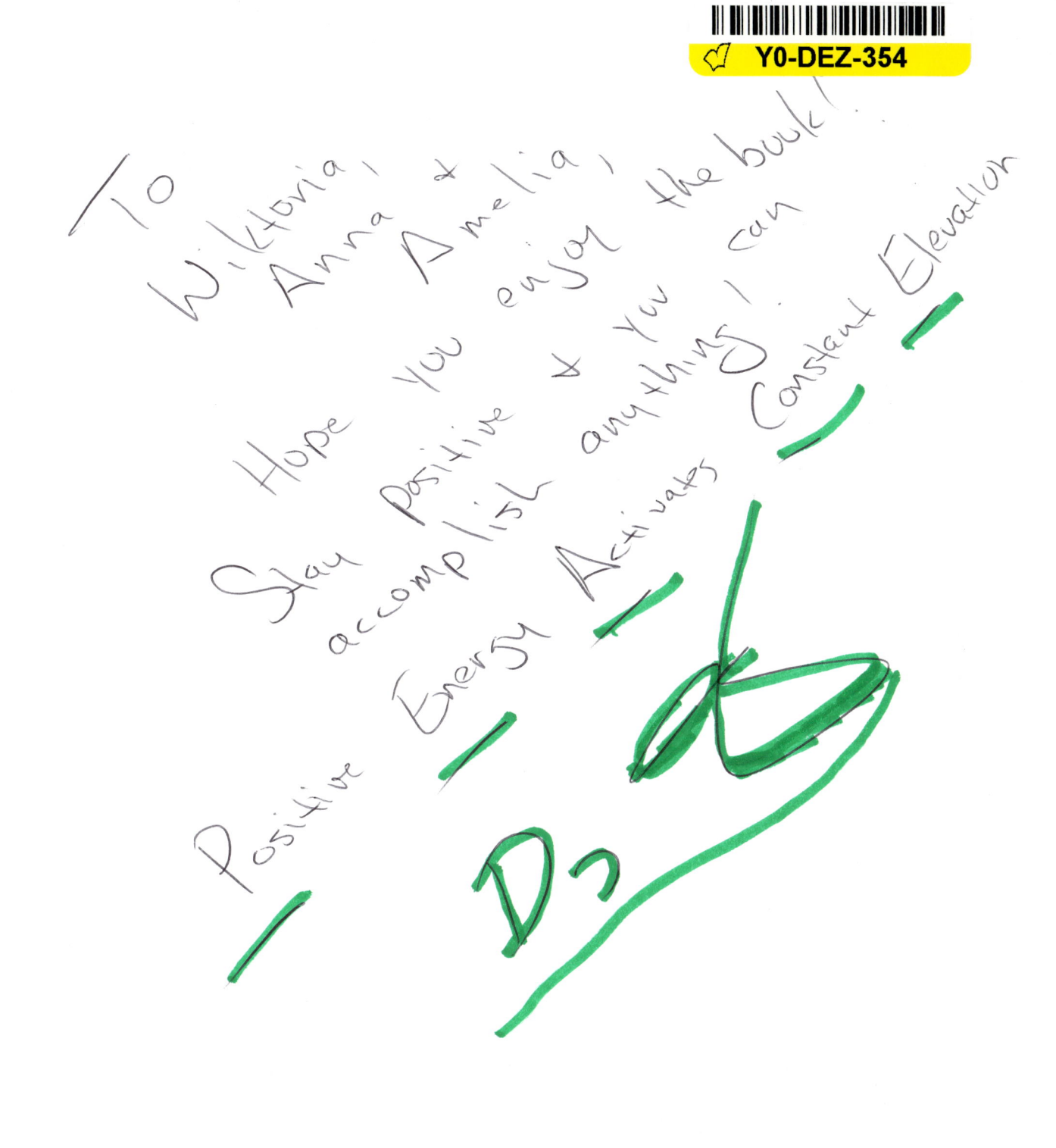

Hope you enjoy the book!

Stay positive & you can accomplish anything!

Positive Energy Activates Constant Elevation

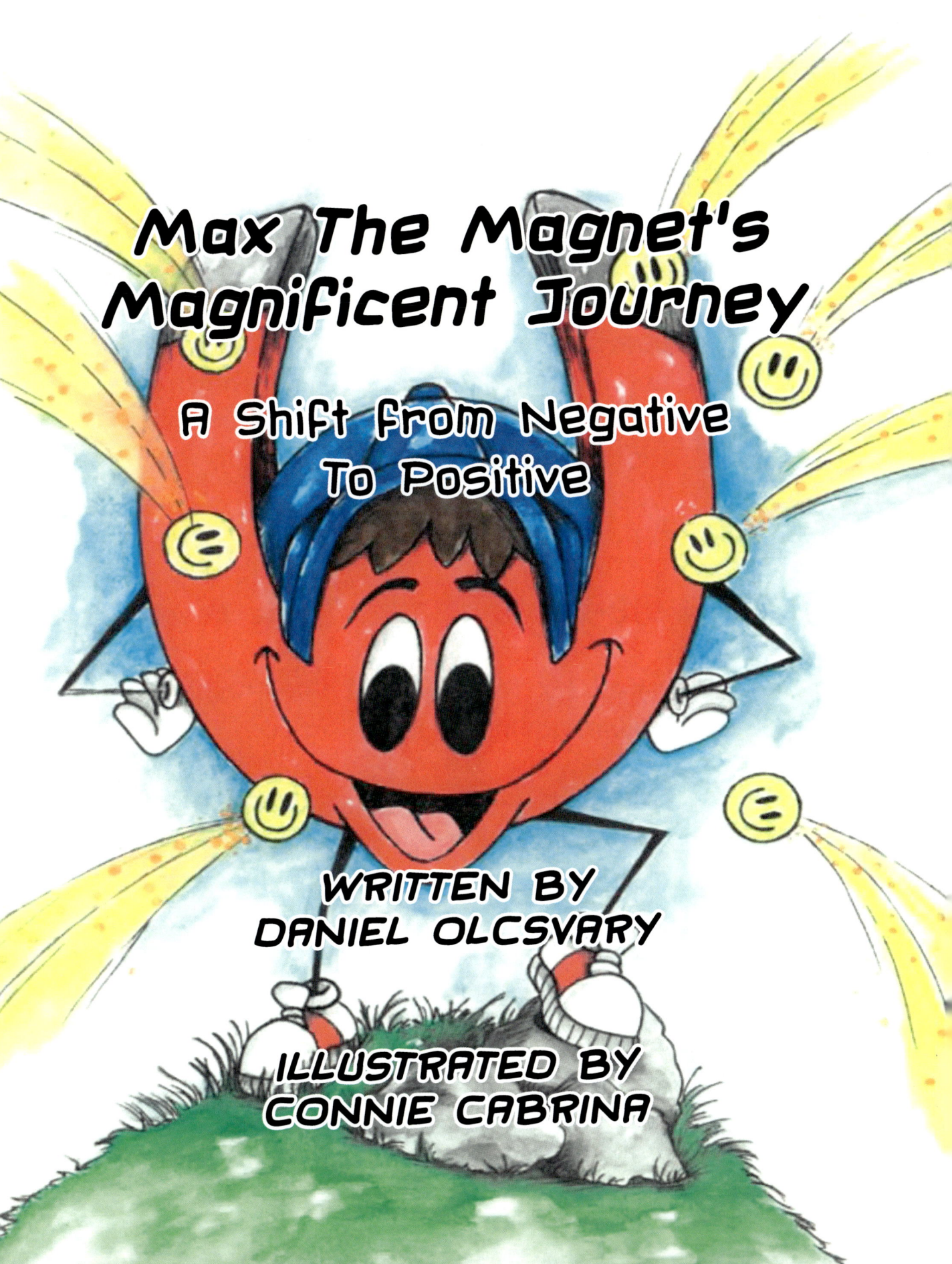

Copyright © 2020 by Daniel Olcsvary

All rights reserved. No part of this book may be reproduced or used in any manner without written permission of copyright owner except for the use of quotations in a book review.

First paperback edition May 2020

ISBN 978-0-578-68841-1 (paperback)

Published by Mind Write Publishing
www.mindwritepublishing.com

Be sure to follow @max_the_magnet on Instagram and follow Mind Write Publishing on Facebook.

For Amilya,

May you attract nothing but positive energy and give the same back to the universe.

Love you,
Daddy

He lives with his mom and his sister,
Maggie the Magnet.

He is always yelling at his mom and Maggie.

When Max couldn't beat the final level of Magna-Fighters, he got so angry he broke his controller!

He tripped and scraped his knee!

When Max arrived at school, he realized his anger had gotten the best of him. He forgot to have his mom sign the permission slip for the class trip to the Magnetic Mines. He would have to spend the day in the principal's office while the rest of his friends had fun on the trip!

Max's body felt like it was on fire! His head felt like it was going to explode! He was overcome by all of this negative energy! He stood up and screamed at the top of his lungs, "I haaaaaate my life!!!!"

Max's guidance counselor, Mr. Magner, called him into his office. He put on some relaxing music and instructed Max to take ten deep breaths with his eyes closed. Max started to feel a little better.

Mr. Magner explained to Max that if he was angry all the time, he was going to attract nothing but negative energy in his life.

Mr. Magner offered some strategies to help. He showed Max some basic meditation exercises and wanted him to try it for five minutes each morning.

Mr. Magner gave Max a "Positive Energy Journal" and wanted him to write three things that made him happy before he left for school each morning.

Mr. Magner also role-played with Max to show him how to talk to someone in a calm, mindful manner when he began to feel angry. He said letting his feelings out like this will make Max feel better. Max looked up to Mr. Magner, so he decided to give the strategies a try.

Max started using Mr. Magner's strategies every morning. As the days went on, he started to notice something; he didn't feel so angry anymore.

Max started talking with his mom more. He even started playing with Maggie!

His gym teacher noticed the change in Max's behavior and invited him to join the basketball team!

His mom was so happy with his behavior that they started doing more fun things as a family!

Max went to visit Mr. Magner's office and was filled with gratitude. "Thank you so much for your help! My life is so much better now, and it is because of you!"

Mr. Magner replied, "You are welcome Max. You should be very proud of yourself. I showed you the way, but you made the journey!"

"Journey?" Max asked. "What kind of journey?"

Mr. Magner smiled and said, "The journey from negative to positive."

Beginner's Meditation/Deep Breathing Exercise

Find a quiet place where you can sit and relax for a few minutes. Sit down in a comfortable position. Close your eyes and try to visualize a beautiful place (a beach, a forest, a park where you like to play, etc.). Breathe in deeply through your nose and in your mind count to five. Hold the breath for another five seconds. Slowly exhale, counting to five in your mind as you release the breath. Repeat this for five minutes as you clear your mind of all negativity and focus on the beautiful image of the scenery in your mind. You can do this activity for more or less time if needed.

POSITIVE ENERGY STARTER KIT

When you wake up in the morning, write down or draw three things that make you happy. It could be things like a certain family member, a special friend, a place you like to eat, or something like a toy or activity that brings you joy. It just has to be something that fills you with positive energy. Have a notebook or paper and some writing utensils in your room each night, so it's easy to do first thing in the morning. Do this activity for five days straight. On the fifth day, draw a picture of how you feel after taking the time to think about what you are happy or grateful for. If you feel this activity helps deal with your anger, start to do this every morning. You can do this in a journal, notebook, or just random pieces of paper.

EXPRESSING YOUR FEELINGS ROLE-PLAY

Imagine this scenario. You have your favorite book in your dresser so no one in your family can touch it. One of your family members comes into your room and borrows your book without your permission. You are fuming with anger! Take ten deep breaths and think about or write down what you would say to that family member. Remember that it is ok to express feelings like anger, but it is the way that you express it that can get you in trouble (hitting, yelling, tantrums, etc.). Think about other feelings you experience and role-play how you express them as well.

BEFORE AND AFTER PICTURES

On a piece of paper draw a picture of how you look and feel when you are angry. Be as descriptive as possible. If you feel like your head is about to explode, draw that explosion!

Now, on the other side of the paper, draw a picture of how you look and feel after you use some of the strategies that Max used in the story. What is different about each picture?

AUTHOR AND ILLUSTRATOR INFO

Daniel Olcsvary has been an early childhood educator for eighteen years, making a positive impact in his classroom on hundreds of students throughout that time. He has also spent the last twelve years in the behavioral field, providing in-home services, and developing coping strategies for children with different behavioral challenges. He is an avid reader and interested in subjects like mindfulness, Taoism, and positive psychology. His personal mantra is "always a student," and he spends his free time watching old school kung fu flicks, listening to golden-era hip hop, making his world-famous guacamole, and learning new things from his beautiful daughter Amilya. This is his first book.

Connie Cabrina has been an illustrator for over twenty-two years. This will be her third children's book and fourth publication in total. She has been working in the school system as an art teacher for over ten years and currently serves at-risk teenagers through artistic outlets.

Made in the USA
Middletown, DE
25 August 2020